My First Book about Camels

Amazing Animal Books
Children's Picture Books
By Molly Davidson

Mendon Cottage Books

JD-Biz Publishing

Read More Amazing Animal Books

Purchase at Amazon.com

Table of Contents

Introduction

Camels have also been called the cars of the desert, for over one hundred years.

They might be a funny looking animal that spits and has a hump.

Really camels are just good at adapting to the desert environment where they live

What is a camel?

There are two types of camels; the Bactrian camel and the dromedary camel.

Two Bactrian camels

They spread their weight out between the third and fourth toes; this is the same as deer, pigs, giraffes, sheep, and goats.

Camel's humps are full of fat storage, when they run out of food or water; their body will start using up the stored fat.

They don't sweat, because they need to keep all the water they drink.

A camel can live for about 50 years.

They have thick eye lashes and also three sets of eyelids, these help keep the sand out of their eyes.

What kinds of camels are there?

A dromedary camel

The first type of camel is called the dromedary camel; they live in Africa and the Middle East.

Dromedary camels only have one hump.

The second type of camel is the Bactrian camel, which lives in Central Asia.

Bactrian camels are better in the cold, like the mountains where they live.

Bactrian camels in front of mountains in Mongolia

Where do camels live?

Camels live in Africa, the Middle East, Central Asia, and in zoos all over the World.

Several camels in Ethiopia

They are best adapted to desert, places with little water, so this is where they tend to live.

Bactrian camels have more fur than dromedary camels, so they can handle the colder deserts better.

The ancestor's of the camel were first started in North America, and then they slowly migrated to Africa and Asia, where they live today.

What do camels eat?

Camels eat plants; in a very interesting way.

A camel grazing

Since camels live in the desert, their bodies absorb all the water from everything they eat, nothing goes to waste.

They have a thick, leathery lining in their mouth as a protection from the thorny desert plants that they eat.

The history of camels and humans

Camels have been helping humans for thousands of years.

There are only a few wild camels that live in the Gobi Desert in Mongolia, the rest are owned by humans.

A caravan of camels

Humans started using camels for transportation, in Africa, over 5,000 years ago.

They started out as a pack animal, which means they hauled humans stuff from one place to another, but then men started using them in wars.

Camel cavalries (army men on camels) are stilled used in Africa, India, and the Arabian Peninsula.

A camel cavalry in Beersheba in 1915

Humans also use camels for their milk, people called nomads, say one can survive on camel's milk, and nothing else, for several months.

They also use their milk to make yogurt, butter, and ice cream.

Humans will also eat the meat from a camel.

What are camelids?

Camelids are like cousins of the camel; these include alpacas, llamas, guanacos, and vicuñas.

A herd of alpacas

An alpaca has soft and warm fur, which is mostly what it is used for.

A vicuña lives wild in the Andes Mountains; they are believed to be the ancestors of the alpaca. They are also the symbol of Peru.

A vicuña in Peru

Llamas are used for their hair, which comes in many different colors.

They are also larger than alpacas, so they are used to carry things from one place to another.

A mother llama with her baby

Guanacos live in the arid mountains of South America.

They all look the same with brown hair covering their bodies, and white underneath.

A Guanacos in Chile

Camelids all have some similar features that make them related, like long thin necks, long legs, big front teeth, soft foot pads, and they all eat plants.

Camelops

The camelops were a type of camel that used to live in North America; it went extinct about 10,000 years ago.

It was similar to the Bactrian camel, but bigger and heavier.

Sergiodlarosa © <u>Wikimedia Commons</u>

Dromedary camel

Dromedary camels have one hump and are used for ridding by many people.

Dromedary camel

They are also called the Arabian or Indian camel.

This type of camel is very fast, and is sometimes used in camel races.

A camel race in the Sahara Desert

The dromedary camel is very gentle, calm, and tough, considering it has to live in the deserts of the Middle East, India, and Africa.

Baby camels have 22 teeth, and adults have 34 teeth (that's two more than an adult human).

To show that they are upset, dromedary camels will snap or stamp their feet at other camels.

They like to walk in a single file line when traveling in a herd.

They make a baaing sheepish sound to find each other, like a wolf howls.

The boys can also whistle through their teeth as a warning.

They chew with their mouths open; and if they get hungry enough will eat fish and drink salt water.

When they walk they move both legs on the same side at the same time, so they swag from one side to the other when walking.

In order for humans to load a camel with stuff, they have to kneel down, because camels are too tall for humans to reach.

Dromedary camel mothers keep their babies inside their bodies for about 15 months until they are born.

The babies will stay with their mother, eating her milk, for about 1 to 2 years.

The dromedary camel is used for meat, milk, and fur.

Bactrian camel

The Bactrian camel lives in the steppes of Central Asia, where there is little water.

They are much rarer than dromedary camels.

A Bactrian camel in Mongolia

They have a lot more hair than the dromedary and have two humps.

There are about 800 wild Bactrian camels in Asia and a few more in Australia, but wild camels are almost extinct.

When a camel has used all the resources it has stored in its humps, they will start to lean to the side.

Like the dromedary, the Bactrian has footpads, nostrils they can close, and thick eyelashes.

Hybrid camels

Bactrian and dromedary camels can breed together; the baby is called an F1.

They usually have one large hump; they also are bigger and stronger than both the Bactrian and dromedary camel.

F1's can also mate with another dromedary or Bactrian making a baby called the F2.

Humans like to race the F2's because they are fast, they also can carry more than the dromedary camels.

Conclusion

These fascinating animals live in our zoos, in the wild, and are a very important for food and transport of nomads throughout Asia and Africa.

There are not as many camels as horses, but they are used by just as many people for transportation, also camels can live in places horses cannot.

Lastly, camels can drink up to 30 gallons, at one time; this takes them about 13 minutes!

Publisher

JD-Biz Corp

P O Box 374

Mendon, Utah 84325

http://www.jd-biz.com/

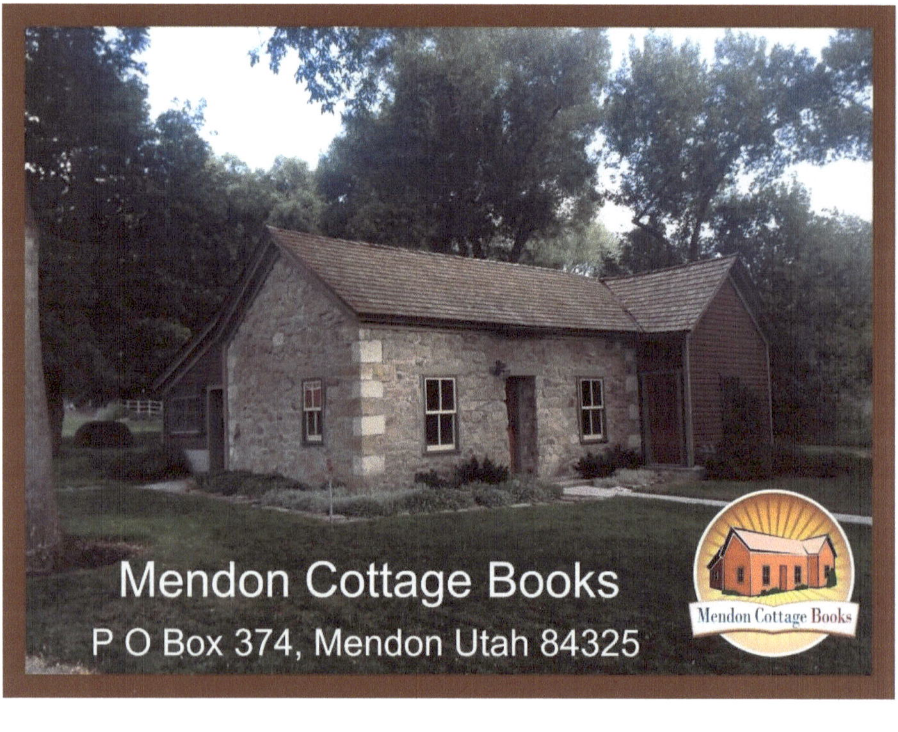

Mendon Cottage Books

P O Box 374, Mendon Utah 84325

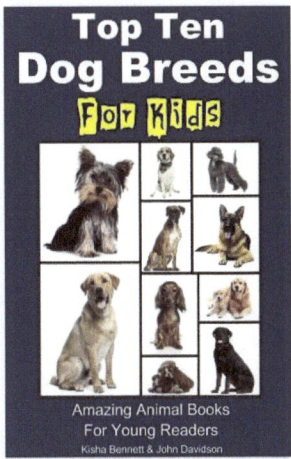

Top Ten Dog Breeds For Kids

Amazing Animal Books For Young Readers

Kisha Bennett & John Davidson

Poodles

Dog Books for Kids

K. Bennett

Labrador Retrievers

Dog Books for Kids

K. Bennett

German Shepherds

Dog Books for Kids

K. Bennett

Rottweilers

Dog Books for Kids

K. Bennett

Boxers

Dog Books for Kids

K. Bennett

Golden Retrievers

Dog Books for Kids

K. Bennett

Beagles

Dog Books for Kids

K. Bennett

Yorkies

Dog Books for Kids

K. Bennett

Our books are available at

1. Amazon.com

2. Barnes and Noble

3. Itunes

4. Kobo

5. Smashwords

6. Google Play Books

Download Free Books!
http://MendonCottageBooks.com

www.ingramcontent.com/pod-product-compliance
Lightning Source LLC
Chambersburg PA
CBHW050859290526
45792CB00002B/665

*9 7 8 1 5 3 0 2 6 0 8 1 2 *